PIONEER VALLEY B

GARDENING

ROSE LEWIS

Here is a garden.

You can grow fruits,
vegetables, and flowers
in a garden.
Fruits, vegetables,
and flowers
grow on plants.

Here are some plants growing in a garden.
The plants need the sun to grow.

The plants need water to grow, too.

Look at the weeds.
Weeds are growing
in the garden.
Weeds can take sun
and water away
from the vegetables.

Look at the peas
in the garden.
It is time
to pick the peas.

Look at the strawberries
in the garden.
It is time
to pick the strawberries.

Look at the vegetables.
The vegetables
are good to eat!

GLOSSARY

plants

flowers

vegetables

fruits

16